TIPS TO HELP YOU DO YOUR BEST

~

RECENT AND SELECTED TITLES FROM TUPELO PRESS

Nebulous Vertigo
Belle Ling

Westminster West
Chard de Niord

Jalousie
Allyson Paty

Mycocosmic
Lesley Wheeler

Phantom Number: An Abecedarium for April
Spring Ulmer

The Last Milkweed
Alan Berolzheimer,
Jeffrey Levine, & Allison O'Keefe, eds.

The Haunting
Cate Peebles

The Radiant
Lise Goett

The Opening Ritual
G.C. Waldrep

Called Back
Rosa Lane

Landsickness
Leigh Lucas

The Right Hand
Christina Pugh

Green Island
Liz Countryman

The Beautiful Immunity
Karen An-hwei Lee

Small Altars
Justin Gardiner

Country Songs for Alice
Emma Binder

Asterism
Ae Hee Lee

then telling be the antidote
Xiao Yue Shan

Therapon
Bruce Bond & Dan Beachy-Quick

membery
Preeti Kaur Rajpal

How To Live
Kelle Groom

Sleep Tight Satellite
Carol Guess

THINE
Kate Partridge

The Future Will Call You Something Else
Natasha Sajé

Night Logic
Matthew Gellman

The Unreal City
Mike Lala

Wind—Mountain—Oak: Poems of Sappho
Dan Beachy-Quick

Tender Machines
J. Mae Barizo

We Are Changed to Deer at the Broken Place
Kelly Weber

Why Misread a Cloud
Emily Carlson

The Strings Are Lightning and Hold You In
Chee Brossy

Ore Choir: The Lava on Iceland
Katy Didden and Kevin Tsang

The Air in the Air Behind It
Brandon Rushton

The Future Perfect: A Fugue
Eric Pankey

American Massif
Nicholas Regiacorte

City Scattered
Tyler Mills

Today in the Taxi
Sean Singer

TIPS TO HELP YOU DO YOUR BEST

~

MIKE CARLSON

TUPELO PRESS
North Adams, Massachusetts

Tips to Help You Do Your Best.
Copyright © 2025 Mike Carlson

ISBN: 978-1-961209-34-3 (paperback)

Library of Congress Control Number: 2025933296
Cataloging-in-Publication data available on request.

Cover and text designed by Ann Aspell.

Cover art: Henri Rousseau, *The Football Players,* Wikimedia Commons | CC BY 4.0
http://creativecommons.org/licenses/by/4.0/

First paperback edition July 2025

All rights reserved. Other than brief excerpts for reviews and commentaries, no part of this book may be reproduced by any means without permission of the publisher. Please address requests for reprint permission or for course-adoption discounts to:

Tupelo Press
P.O. Box 1767
North Adams, Massachusetts 01247
(413) 664-9611 / Fax: (413) 664-9711
editor@tupelopress.org
www.tupelopress.org

Tupelo Press is an award-winning independent literary press that publishes fine fiction, non-fiction, and poetry in books that are a joy to hold as well as read. Tupelo Press is a registered 501(c)(3) non-profit organization, and we rely on public support to carry out our mission of publishing extraordinary work that may be outside the realm of the large commercial publishers.
Financial donations are welcome and are tax deductible.

for May

"the divine wife, the sweet, eternal, perfect comrade"

CONTENTS

THE DAILY PRACTICE OF MAKING POEMS

CONTINUOUS WORK IN THE RIGHT WAY

THEORY AND PRACTICE OF LANDSCAPE POETRY

THE DAILY PRACTICE OF MAKING POEMS

~

Tips to Help You Do Your Best

What is helpful is wine and knowing how
    to tune the bottom string of your guitar by listening to
    a car door slam and adjusting for
        the make and model.

Otherwise, stones line a broken hillside.
    Oak trees extend in all directions.
Scientific case studies rejecting the value of multivitamins
    keep coming out.

It's early still. As long as you're alive and well,
    shoplifting remains an option.
Life is hard and people are feeble and birds mash down
    the corners of an empty box of raisins.

The end of the day should be down there somewhere
    below the fire escape or behind that wall
    of purple canisters.

The end of the day should be something you can draw
    in detail like a pinecone.

Hospice, North Dakota

I'm not sure if this is a town.
    The stores don't sell a single thing a dying person needs.
Every couple hours, the slanting trees lean closer to the ground.
    In a few days, they'll be down.
Wet roots drying over pits the state will use as graves.

Dying people need bicycles to assemble in darkness,
    or jobs writing instructions for self-pulling lawnmowers,
    or antlers rising from the tall brown
        grass that stretches back toward the bandshell.
They need to know the state won't bury them in a hole left
    by the failure of a tree.

And trees can't fail. Only men and women.
    Only towns, if that's what this place is,
and towns can only fail if the reservoir reflects the condos on the hill
    in some weird, unfortunate way that highlights how cheap
    the siding is and makes them hard to sell.

Only an exhausted bird would nest here chest high
    between signs for two stores that failed in this strip mall.
Only a bird tortured by storm who watched her mate
    give up mid-air and drop to the cornfield
    below like a wine bottle.

Wrong flecks the landscape like cheap insulation.
    Wrong oak tree, wrong car door, wrong mailbox, wrong joke.
There are reasons why people try heroin.
    Real reasons that camping can't resolve, or art, or getting
    a job at the cemetery.

Gross Cove

Does the sky mean more to the fox than the jellyfish?
    These stacks of dead cod separated by magazine covers
    don't convince me either way.

But the marina parking lot is almost empty.
    A seagull follows the shortest path possible through a rubble
    of asphalt and triangular clam shell.
Old docks destroyed by rain slant down into dark green water.

There was a time in the Great Salt Lake of my purposes
    when I went around repeating
    the phrase, "Boating is not okay."

But no longer. The confidence that came with that
    cynicism has retreated into the tower
    in my nightmares I can't enter.
A clacking of metal eggs, a reticent whimpering,
    but the door doesn't open.

Picture an anorexic butterfly being operated on by
    a maple leaf holding a scalpel,
    that's what I do.
I am like a child who has been caught in a second lie and is preparing
    a third that his exasperated teacher
    won't even listen to.

And boating is fine. Spend the day considering
    the psychological consequences of refusing
    to wear a life preserver.
Stare at a compass. Keep saying "starboard" until the vowel sounds
    blur and you have no idea how
    it would look scrawled out on parchment.
Decide things, that's what I do.
    If I ever become an arsonist, for instance,
    I will concentrate mostly on lighthouses.

Flexicore vs. Durastone

I have no idea. When I was young, Craig MacMillan and I would ride
to a restaurant in the back of my father's station wagon
while our parents sat up front discussing
the relative merits of old money and the nouveaux riche.
Craig was four years older than me and could recite
the lyrics of songs I'd never heard and apply
them to the landscape in a way that made me admire
his axiomatic tone.

Along the way, we'd pass an isolated factory, sitting like an enormous
upturned brick on one side of the highway, windowless,
the strange word Durastone across the top of one side,
Flexicore across the other.

Craig would argue Durastone was stronger of the two,
and pound a fist into his hand, and clench his teeth
to make his point.
I had no idea what I was saying, but I tried to make the case that Flexicore
was like a sapling bending in a storm while branches
of the larger Durastone-like trees blew past, destroyed
because they couldn't yield.

I tried to match the tone my father took when he expressed disdain
for the nouveaux riche who he firmly believed
were not as savvy as old money.
None of us had any idea what we were talking about or why,
but the sound of our voices was the strength that we had in a landscape
where Durastone and Flexicore were one, and the rich
were one, and the power that we had came
from disagreeing with each other.

Youth and Buddhist Activism

I weep for what the objects in my suitcase reveal about my practice,
the novels I can't finish, Villette, Middlemarch, and my ex-wife's diary
in which she decides at no real length to leave me.

I grew up down the road from the Providence Zen Center,
but it was Annathena Moon who taught me how to do zazen
in her bedroom after school below a David Bowie poster.

I did not mistake her nipples for whatever they were pointing at.
I counted three and one-half breaths before I leapt at her.

More than once I have mistaken meditation for opportunity.

More than once I have puttered around the Emerald Square Mall
during the Super Bowl, adrift with no reliable role model,
convinced that even Master Hongdau is a slut, has balls,
ejaculates on the Buddha's face nightly manifesting sorrow.

All buddhas and bodhisattvas feel rejected by the moon
and they walk home drunk trying to leave a trail of broken mailboxes.

Occasionally they are tackled by teenage do-gooders into a vegetable garden
and pass out reaching for an eggplant to defend themselves with.

More than once I have woken up to the sound of my cold body
being dragged through a mortar of beets, sorrel, okra, and chicken wire.

I've cried out to the boy who is dragging me, and each time he's stopped,
I've noticed that his t-shirt has a barbell on it and it says, "God's Gym."

More than once this boy in the weight-lifting t-shirt has asked me
if I am willing to accept Jesus Christ as my personal savior.

But I've always said no, I've said thank you, that's kind of you, no.
This path that we've torn through the tarragon is not a mistake.

Ways Out of an Apple Orchard

I should have left by now, turned back where the odor
    of wood glue met a whiff of dead oak tree.
I should have chased some laughter down the hill and said hello,
    whoever stood there, whatever hair, whatever color
    sweater.

Everyone here drove, but there are other ways to leave.
    I could use the blue tarp as a map and try
    to find a lake that has a rip in every corner.
I could call the scarecrow north and walk southwest
    until I see an injured pony crumpled in a stream or find
    a fallen motorcycle inside a tunnel.

I don't need a farmhand to tell me I'm a dud.
    Sky and hay do that.
Sky and hay advance a hatred of my hair, my plans, my life
    as if their steep critique was just a folksy gesture.

There is a trick to lifting up a fallen motorcycle alone.
    The key is stooping down and sweeping away the gravel.
Midway through the lift, you can tell a lot about your self
    by how much noise your boots make.

Man Hitting Golf Balls into a Cemetery

Before a single crow decorating the dogwood to my right was able
to lay his eyes on the source of the plink and the subsequent
thud, I had already discovered and forgiven the idiot.

I don't know if he was trying to get better at golf
or worse at life, but the condition
of his house, or more likely, his parents' house, across the street
from the cemetery, and the piles of torn
shingle on the porch, and the damaged
antelope lawn statue, relieved me of any generic
outrage.

I watched him use the toe of a long iron to gather
a golf ball from the overturned bucket
and balance it gingerly, almost
conscientiously, on a quarter tuft of crabgrass.

It was still a long shot from his barren front
yard to the smooth black arms of the limestone angel.

Solo Exhibition

Christ took three photographs of hell.
In one, a uniform gray rubble of cups, concrete, two-by-fours, and clothing
accentuates the pure black mouth of a shaving kit beside
an empty can of spray paint.

In another, an old man climbs the mangled staircase
of an abandoned jail whose walls
have been covered to mask their ruin.
What the plastic does not hide reveals how silly it was
to put the plastic up at all.

The last one is a view from the roof of the brewery.
Looking down on the city, you can see the largest building
used to hold a clock face or some kind
of seal, but now there is only a stain, or lack of sun, a darker
circle demanding your hypothesis.

How odd that the women who enter the cathedral must do so
in a paper shawl as if their shoulders said more
about sorcery than their faces.
Sunlight lands on the steps of their forearms
and climbs them informally
like insect or wine.

A Diagram of the Inca Road System

I don't pray for rain, I put it there.
    Men wash plates in sludge I brighten
    with a yellow crayon.
Below the rope bridge that connects two sets
    of jaguar tracks, inept messengers can't get bonfires started.
There's a bicycle beside the temple.
    I had a snake there first then changed it to a handlebar.

In the next few years, I plan to remember what
    my mother said when I asked her what a douche bag was.
I plan to write that definition down and ask the first engraver
    I can find what object it should live on.

Then I will devote my diagram to praise.
    In what the Sapa Inca does, I'll find great delicacy.
By noting how sunlight hits the packing tape
    he used to fix the temple floor, I'll suggest
    his oafish ways are holy.

From then on, whatever wood I find beside me
    in the darkness of my room or by the river, I'll make into
    a chair I learn to play the panpipe in.
I'll ask the high priest what a douche bag is.
    I know the moon is not one.

Museum of Ham

In Spanish, everything closes.
    The eyes of pigs collapse around an image
    of a farmer lifting clean Islamic stone.
Newspapers shut down at noon so a reporter can gather up a cat
    into his antiseptic palm and toss it from a wide
    ceramic roof.
Wine finds men sleeping at a beautiful hospital.

When I came here to visit my sister at business school, I also
    shut down.
It was two weeks after the surgery I had to close off
    a network of dilated veins near my testicles.
I didn't want to meet her classmates or discuss my favorite
    products or explain the bag of worms
    inside my scrotum.
I didn't want to attend a lecture on financial virility
    in which no one cared what was being created or why.

When the Italian woman spoke lovingly
    about Proctor & Gamble, I made my way
    to the museum because I know what journeys are and how
        to tell them from vacation.

I walked back and forth in front of Goya's Third of May.
    I studied the Spanish captives about to be slaughtered,
    the eyes of the man in the white shirt
        with his arms stretching out, with his whole life
        exposed to the soldiers' huge lantern.
I wanted to hold out my arms to my sister.
    The stiches on my abdomen tore secretly open.

Comedy vs. Casual Joke Telling

Did I actually sit there? Yes. I wore my brother's jean jacket
    and my sister's fingerless gloves.
It was overcast and fall.
    The smell of rotting pumpkin agitated the squirrels.
    I tried to focus.

You see, the joke teller has no real politics.
    He has friends he can count on and always feels
    he might have played at least one sport semi-professionally.
        The gist of any song is enough for him.

If you want to be funny, however, in a deep way
    like the apostles or a large oak tree separating two gas stations,
    then everything that happens to you must happen
        over and over, and you must keep making arbitrary distinctions
        until one of them rings unexpectedly true.

The Total Hopeless Catastrophe of Time

To gaze at the protesters climbing a pyramid
    is like listening to horns and sirens separate.
In the distance, cranes lift beams to the top
    of cylindrical buildings.
Clouds are smoke from things we set on fire.
    Pigeons, smoke from rooftops.

Tigers this close to town keep killing dogs and end up in zoos.
Sweaters this close to the riverbank
    turn up in photographs.
Garbage trucks are snow plows all winter.
    Trees are armatures we walk toward with boxes of clay.

There is no culmination.
    At the top of the pyramid, the pyramid ends.
A few days later, the river is brown again.
    The sun is a survey we answer by pressing
    our lips to the arm of a girl on a poster.

Beware of Ideas

You are tired of writing in green pen about Sacagawea's arm hair.
You are tired of using the swallows and the melon planet
to predict the actions of the moving men.

But suddenly you have something in common with all
your ancestors: a daughter.
All of Shakespeare and psychotherapy is now
immediately available to you.

The moving men may have patented semen, but astonishment
no one can copyright.
You no longer have need of a codex.
You no longer need to study the black square
or ceramic cylinder.

The best parts of Paradise Lost are where Milton writes about himself,
even Samuel Johnson suggested that, so why don't you stop
trying to write a poetic sequence about the military equivalent of
Lewis and Clark and get back to the issue
of your own exceeding blindness.

Thematic Prayer for a Scholarly Monotone

What the sage wrote, however true,
      however fat the sage was, or blind,
      matters little in the pink fluorescence
            laid up on this windowless wall.
Sunlight is and isn't bent
      over eight indicative paint drips,
      meaningful, as all errors are,
            telling of the worker, the work.

In this great silence, this brute light,
      whose totem groin is nothingness,
      the soul is awed by minor surfaces,
            whatever the sage wrote, however true.
The eyelash of that vanished girl
      who cursed at the librarian
      rocks gently in a path of dust
            missed by the custodian's rag.

Exile

Whole afternoons in these beige motels,
America, I studied my fly-swatting, asthmatic self,
and prepared a conversation between the beach
dust and its watercolor crab.

I, Mike Carlson, writer of goodbye letters, iridescent
in the waffle light under palms
the size and shape of snow shoes, will off and on answer to Patriot,
my country people, though I see
where mangoes hit the far rock wall and fragment
on the backs of fishermen.

Tell me, middle-class, earmuffed America, unskilled
students of marijuana and touchdown celebrations,
where is your emotional boundary?

Why have you driven me off among mangroves
to annotate my grandfather's address book
and conceive a small ode to this trash bag of dead
mouse, forsythia, and orange peel?

The great war which is part of my prayer, more
and more sincere, the further I get from you,
the war against Orpheus, against mention
of Orpheus, against allusion to Orpheus,
or Ovid, or weeping, will never be fought in the beard of your grain,
the oceans of soft hair capping
hazel high stalks, or the down of your husks,
your hierarchies of floss.

I never look back and still you are not with me.

CONTINUOUS WORK IN THE RIGHT WAY

~

Love Song

so that's what it is

that the little rectangular notes on the cork board
    are no longer relevant

that the nautical chart with my father's pencil markings
    is inaccurate as to the depths of my sorrow

that this is no inconsequential assemblage
    this lopsided tower of books on the dresser
    whose foundation is a tiny edition of Antony and Cleopatra
    whose mortar is a book mark
    a dollar bill and three pieces
    of junk mail all squeezed somewhat out the sides and balancing
    over my car keys and wallet

that the cord from the printer is loosely draped
    over two bent sheets of copy paper

that my adrenalin shot and inhaler foreground a bottle of hand sanitizer

that one half of the long cardboard box for the baby gate
    is beside me like a close friend at a funeral

that the small statue of a bronze hound hovers midstep
    looking backward over the dish containing two wristwatches
    that you and I no longer wear

Ball Song

After Christopher Smart

yet I signal my students to silence by call and response
and by clapping and lying to them
for the makers of balls deal in textures

yet I remain colloquial in my resentment of initiatives
for the bouncing of balls is a requiem

yet I send my shoes off in a box to be resoled at a cost
that would embarrass my father
for all notes played on a drum are balls in the head of the hearer

yet I have a brother Steve to whom my silence must seem pride
and my conscience upon reflection prove it
for all things that roll you would not call a plaything

yet the names of goldfish and rock bands
are also the names on arrest warrants
for a great sport that requires two balls still escapes us

yet ventriloquism is the spirit's reckoning with jargon
for a ball in a cell is a blessing

Outskirts

1

In summer, I'd walk to the old tower
and lift
a heavy crate so I could observe
the bent grass unmesh
and intershelve.
The runways were always bare except for
four old nuns
                    who would gather themselves there
to gossip about
God's strength. The five
of us would stop
to watch
a turtle dove
dart through the long, empty airplane hangar.

2

I walked through the marsh because I wanted
a shovel
from the large barn, and even
though the air
was tar, the ghost of the sun
on the side of the hay
                    stroked my forehead
and hair like a calm, honest wife would.
The best art of any farm
isn't corn
or grain, but
the sparse,
electric, mortal sheen
on things you pass while walking to a shed.

3

Winter is the safest place to grow psalms.
Between the lake
and the church, a young man slaps
his shovel on the dirt
to even
out the mound. At dawn, he found two swans
dead
        from cold and went home to put on jeans.
Now he pets
the dappled
grass to clean
his hands. He dunks
his father's shovel in
the creek until its worn depression gleams.

4

The sleepy chicken eavesdrops on a pair of
flames that
flirt with a cinderblock.
The fire
that destroyed the old church
has dwindled, but there
is still a list of things
                                    a good chicken would love
to see burn in the first spring shadows of
homeless lilac. Turning
toward the door
where they used to sell
blue soap shaped like star-
fish, I list each thing I think I have.

Barn Song

whereas lights from the cable modem flash lightly on the torn flap
    of an old bag of horse supplement

whereas the full length mirror I leaned on the mowstead wall
    still wears the ChapStick impression of lips
    where I kissed myself weeks ago

whereas I am climbing the built-in ladder adjacent to the wagon bays
    up onto the principal rafter of happiness

my view of the river is obstructed by pulley attachments

Dirge

I remember her rabid and yellow with cheetah spots walking
slowly in the other direction

I remember her inflatable and engulfed in flames and stone-eyed
drying out and dying like a plant you forgot to water
then watered too much

I remember her dimpled like a golf ball
squat and accordion-torsoed

I remember her face falling like ash off a cigarette
her fur getting snagged on the wheel of a lawnmower

I remember her back legs stopped working and she pawed herself forward
like a zombie

I don't remember if she was male or female
or two-thirds horse or knew how to play any instruments

I didn't sketch her rib cage in charcoal
or shoot any video to overdub with inner monologue

Two Poems for an Envelope

1

It's the first day of school in the City
of New York, and I'm tempted
to forevow
what is futureful, but a day
is no
wee domino, and each cloud in the sky
outmilks the sky of what
                                        is most pearly
in its beer belly. I also
must go,
shortly. The cross-eyed
and orphaned
must go.
All poems that end true end mid prophecy.

2

Let the beige hay baffle my old sense of
October's color scheme
and the loose fog chase snails through
milk crates.
The saint with his dog
can contradict my definitions of
poetry. There's still art left.
                                        It's enough
that my good wife
hasn't tired of giving
me nicknames.
Nature goes on
making
stairs up a cliff with the bones of a wolf.

Song of My Best Self

for I have given too much of my life to the spirit who
        would be good at things only by practicing
for there must be another spirit who is a natural
        who was raised by rhododendrons in concentric moonlight

for in light of my anger at coworkers
for those who are so wrong that no one explains their errors to them
for the moron with unfathomable self-confidence
        with only the borrowed syntax of humor
        without one toothpick or prayer bead or clover leaf of humility
for his authentic counterpart in a heap in the bathroom sobbing
for the birds still silent days after the explosions
        still wary and unpatriotic and sad
        I have given too much power to premises

for the trees hang from the earth
for I look up at them and remove my glasses
for there are no individual leaves only wet blurs and rough clumps
        only vague glands
        pretentious growth
        heaps of woven fuzz

for dawn is a clean time
for no one can instruct me out of which practices to extract
        what it means to be good or present or sane

for I am not Walt Whitman
for I reject volume and democracy
for I veto satisfaction in favor of collecting driftwood

for if you walk out with me on the beach just north of Esterillos
        I will exhaust your interest in me
for I am like the mysterious cows drowsing on the sand where the beach turns
        in below the milk trees
for my loose fat is a robe for my bent skeleton
for it is almost too much for me to lift my head even at danger

for the rusty refrigerators men have tossed along the shore don't bother me
for I have no plans to remove or recycle them
for they are as natural as the rocks or the reeds for which I take no responsibility
for who needs me to say the earth has been mishandled

Half Day

The results of that pregnancy test were everywhere.
    The wind began to sag. Boys pelted
    a tree house with packets of barbecue sauce.
In the graveyard, some daffodils slipped off
    an obelisk and landed on
    rose petals pressed in a frame.

I had wanted to strum a dead fern and invent
    a new category.
I had wanted to take a swig of whatever
    was in the tulips.

Peppermint Tea Ceremony

The first thing is to be here glistening
    in pajama pants and a black and gray sweater
    with a hole in the armpit.
And by glistening
    I don't mean wet or sparkly,
    I mean alive, balanced precariously
    between two translucent memories
    of a horse stable, and not trying
    to clarify the smell of a fence or remember
    the name of the horse who rode
    up the hill with your heart and your lungs
    pressed flat underneath the weight
    of its saddle.

Be here beside the black refrigerator.
    Be exceedingly here like a man whose wife of fifty years
    just appeared in his dream and chewed on a milk carton.
Be here between the opacity of a backache
and the transparency of an ulcer.
    Be reluctantly here.
        Be temporary.

Things I Will and Won't Forgive Volkswagen

The two women I loved when I moved to this city
	enjoyed chastising their rabbi for driving a Volkswagen.

They were like American troops occupying an auto plant.
	They were like clouds that were years
	that were bones that were thought bubbles.

I was in awe of that kind of morality.
	I hoped they would see it through wherever it led, but it led to them
	rolling their eyes at me for drinking a Coca-Cola.

And Volkswagen isn't a person. If I die early from excess ozone
	or particulate pollution, I'm willing to let that go.

It's downhill to the bay from here and then flat
	water until the hull of the first miserable containership.

A green light lands on the side of a telephone pole
	and lives there like rain that has finally
	caught up with a salamander.

Half Staff

The purpose of the Pledge of Allegiance keeps changing.
Bus routes change, but still they go by twenty
flag poles with a broken pulley.

There are things to throw a rock at on this road
if you are careful, if you believe abandoned barber shops
are evil, if you can manufacture outrage
at a fence post falling over.

On the bus that aims itself at the cemetery
then misses, the faces of teachers and nurses resolve
into a pile of chalk gray stones.

Rain helps us remember snow, and snow
gave us a chance to see a paw land in the center
of a boot print.

Etiquette

For a long time, I got up before my dreams
        had ended, but now I wait to see
        the apple in the starling's mouth.

The morning air presses down with its heel until
        the dew says fine and rises slowly.

Slow is what the dew is good at.

Education and Pretend

Giving up on the spirit of brotherhood, I walk
        toward the park where only the people
        are sad and bees don't worry about
                not having skulls.

The trees follow rules.
        The clouds conform to moods that people on the grass
        arrange by leaning.

Eventually, I want to belong to the ring of stones
        that line the dog pond.
I want to grow a fang I can tongue while measuring
        a width of broken sound.

On the singed grass where a good man set himself
        on fire and died, a volleyball net now lays its shadow
        like the grid of a calendar with too many days.

Dark clouds march toward the museum.
        Clouds with human wings and teeth that no insect
        will ever be born with.

Grand Army Plaza

Fountain water evaporates less quickly than rain.
    It has experienced triumph and can't just let
    itself go like a regular puddle.

Victory affects me similarly.
    I congratulate myself on successful condolences.

That's why I walk around this little park
    apprenticing myself to whatever makes a U-turn.
Sparrows that flit in and out of the armpits of statues.
    Squirrels that find stones to reverse themselves on.

I want to hang up my body like a braided oval rug
    and beat all the gusto out
    of its concentric wool pattern.

Venn Diagram

Differences are easy. The ones that matter
    keep identical twins from climbing a tree in exactly
    the same way.

In any case, I don't chew gum. The rapid loss of flavor
    is way too accurate a metaphor for why I have no patience
    with friendship.

And in the evening, I'm obsessed with other stuff.
    I love the cows on milk cartons.
I love to kick a raspy ball of fuzz beneath the tree in which
    I've seen a possum and a falcon.

Resolution

The end of the year is illusory.
    By that time the Formica and white enamel that I love
    will be replaced by granite and stainless
        steel which trouble me.
Coins I've stacked for months on the windowsill will be knocked
    down by cats I agree to take care of.

Everything human is January.
    Accidental overdose, chance fall from stepladder.
The grass is a wrist that I pin to my calendar.

The dead are not real. They are liable to crumble
    like oyster crackers crunched underfoot in their cellophane packaging.
Only the living are rude. Only the living make ghosts
    from blue and green construction paper and tape them
    on doors to be blanched by the afternoon sun.

The shadows my coworker put down were cast
    by a mountain of tinfoil robots he modeled
    on the adjustable table beside his deathbed.
"Read your best students' writing most carefully," his skin
    said, "Don't live in a house without stairs."

Each year, I walk past the supermarket, thinking
    of pamphlets I've been handed at funerals, of blood cells
    that have disbanded.
I forget the loopholes in my coworker's pension and the slurs
    in my coworker's will.

The stones of the municipal building pale, then redden, then glisten,
    then dim.
I want to glisten and dim.
    What I am after with my choice of sneaker is the life of the hell raiser,
    the life of the beekeeper, the stoic, the dud.

Why I Teach in a Def Leppard T-shirt

Philosophers don't discuss clouds.
    They're professionals.
They investigate the meaning of gang signs in preschool and try
    to pop bubbles that drift into office buildings.

But why bring this up? There is a gong
    by the road outside the Zen center that the track team
    on its five mile run is always going to ring.

There are packets of sun that follow a spider down a rock wall
    and stick, if only suddenly, to a wet leaf lining the dent
    in a deflated soccer ball.

There is gauze. There were bees.
    There are clouds.

Connoisseurship for Aficionados

1

I think of my poems as a family of toadstools
trying to escape America. My subject matter
is the absurd swag an innocent child collects
at a boat show.
I don't seek to make work that prioritizes
certain kinds
of insects or ranks rivers.
My poems are a record of what I had to go on.
My current project, "How to Win at Poetry," is what happens
when I keep writing.

2

The challenge is to lift the dead branches over my head and
make them look like they are still part of the living tree.
My subject matter is nostalgia and how it props up injustice and apathy.
I've always had an affinity for inserting aquariums
into poems about jail time and safe cracking.
My work for the last twenty years has been trying to convert
shame into something more useful like scissors
or air-conditioning.

3

My stanza shape implies a critical view of participation.
It is as though my life and my work are sisters
fighting over who gets to read which magazine at the doctor's
office.
I think of my poems as dice.
My subject matter is shadow and the canister it retreats to
in a rainstorm after an office party.
I've always had an affinity for repeated phrases.

4

I’ve always had
an affinity for wallpaper.
    My subject matter
is abstraction and how it helps
distinguish between irony
and irreverence.
I think of my poems as incomplete
hindsight.

5

It is as though my line length and my integrity
were two parts of a tombstone, the slab
with my name on it and, above it, a sculpture
of a big stupid bear.
My current project, “How to Survive a Mass Shooting,”
is what I think about at outdoor concerts
and movie theaters.
I do not seek to make work that implies fatherhood
is or isn’t a kind of cowardice.
I do not seek to make work that interrogates itself
only to allow the initial suppositions to remain
in the final version.

I Write Poems Like This Now

Last night, I dreamed I was buying a dress shirt,
but I couldn't articulate to the man what kind of stripe
I wanted. I kept saying, "Heathery," and I woke up
feeling like my soul
was a moron, like Carl Jung was shaking his head
at my subconscious dismissively.
It was a dream about unsuccessfully purchasing a dress shirt
and I will carry that depravity up and down
    whatever corridors the wind drives through me
    always.

So from now on,
I only want to write if I can find myself in rags
    wandering an abandoned city where all the windows
        are blown out and cinders
            keep falling. I want to meander past
                inscrutable rubble and hoist myself up
                    through the incinerated chasses of bread trucks.
                    I want to stand for an hour in a fog
                of soot until a drone comes down and hovers
                six inches in front of my face. I want to feel
                the hum of its motor, and let its tiny
                propellers blow the ash out of my eyebrows.
        I want to follow that drone out of the city
        until color returns to the sky and the side of a red barn
        has a blue smudge on it, until Carl Jung looks up
        from the sheep
he is shearing and nods at what's left
of my outfit approvingly.

The Days Ahead

If I follow my thinking back far enough I can see where I began to wonder
why it took so long for me to notice that my finger was bleeding.
All summer I had drawn these pictures of Wallace Stevens. One or two
    kind of looked like him, but when I tried to make
    his mouth like that again, it didn't work
    and I quit before I had him hunched forward
    in a pink suit laughing or sobbing in a green tie
    with a dog on it. Some people have the kind of personality
    that can carry a poem, but my poems need a child
    throwing plastic cars and trucks from a fourth story window.
    My poems need the sound of each toy
    making its way through an enormous oak tree,
    clonking hollowly, branch to branch, then catching briefly
    in a sash of leaves and acorns before smacking
    my hand in the courtyard below.

The Way of the Chinese

After Tu Fu

In college, I was given a list of bullet points
on a sheet of copy paper that said, "The Way of the Chinese."
It was the only way anyone ever explained to me
and I followed it into the woods
behind apartment buildings, into schools
whose walls are plaster that crumbles
like detergent, into staff meetings where recently
dead coworkers were not even mentioned.

If I follow it now, rain knocks lightly
on the top of the air conditioner outside my window
and a sickle of orange
moonlight trembles in an L-shaped puddle
on the sidewalk below.

And while none of this is necessary,
my resistance to reckon with any of it
is as floppy and green as a clue.
What I hate about my poetry
is the sound of an antelope horn being held down
under a work boot.
I can't stand watching myself try to saw
off the remaining bits of fur with the teeth
of a small plastic comb.

But sometimes, when I am having trouble
breathing or drafting a condolence note,
and no one can fill any of my prescriptions,
and a virus is moving across the earth
toward me, newspaper by newspaper,
like an advertisement for a gravestone
that gets larger and larger as I turn

the loud pages, I set down my lists
of particulars and go stand by the light near the sink
in the kitchen. I take the long spout of the faucet
in my cold right hand and move it back and forth
as though it were a tiller.

THEORY AND PRACTICE OF LANDSCAPE POETRY

~

"A man with a hazel wand came without sound;
He changed me suddenly; I was looking another way;
And now my calling is but the calling of a hound;"

—WILLIAM BUTLER YEATS

"And plentitude of plan shall not suffice."

— GWENDOLYN BROOKS

"And now my fears, they come to me in threes . . ."

— JULIAN CASABLANCAS

Zen Mound, Beginner's Mound

In a field this flat, this late, this tranquil
and unevenly mowed, under a sky as sincere
as it is blank, it's clear why people
make sculpture. Any help we can get orienting ourselves
between two roads is good against depression.
In the distance, a seam of pale green mountains
joins a tiny fence to assert that the earth
and the atmosphere have their own personalities.
This is how far away from us the horizon
always is. You're this far from a rental car, this far
from a garbage can, this far from a seesaw
and a swing set. If you're midway between
a hay bale and a windmill, this is exactly how scared
we'd expect you to be.
In the distance, a train horn gives up.
Something is burning in a canister
beside the water tower. It might be a handful
of obsolete electronics, or a cereal box,
or a map with a dragon on it. It might be
a detective novel, a refrigerator manual, a handbook
on how to teach grammar.
There's a place you can be at in a poem
where a barn has only one side, where the air
catches a sheet of plywood in the back
of a speeding pick-up truck and lifts it
into the air, holding it lightly, decently,
until it tilts of its own weight and comes down
vertically, violently into the hood
of an old blue station wagon.
There's a place you can be at in a poem
where the next thing you say will break
your daughter's heart, or her guinea pig's spirit,
or confirm for your father how fitfully
three sparrows stand along a fence post.
This is how far away from us
the horizon always is.

Zen Apology, Beginner's Apology

By wholeheartedly, I mean I'm sorry in a way
that audits even stones for bruises, a way
that sits in the park on a shower curtain.
Looking for help with my tone and my need
to overexplain my silence, I'm seeking concrete
and unpleasant laughter at a tray
of my collected condolence notes.

There are so many things I'm exceedingly
worse than: fog, Maine, rhyme, cafeteria noise, etc.
I want to be at least as good as the baby clothes
of the abandoned child
the nurses nicknamed Billy Sunshine and which
a police inspector reported
were "clean and of medium quality."
I vow to be clear as day, completely
accessible, like a bag of bagels torn open
by birds, like the dates on the back
of a concert t-shirt.

Zen Wind, Beginner's Wind

I started in April, the sun not yet
a small bronze paperweight, the sea not yet
a blue-gray welt in the shakiness of my lower-left eyelid.
Architects and nurses out
walking their dogs. Mortgage brokers out
listening at the larger bushes
for proof of sparrows. Every few minutes
a huge gust of wind would make a man
reach up and press his baseball cap against
his forehead. And then, what might have been
the sound of someone untangling wooden wind chimes
from the bars of a fire escape became
a milk crate tumbling into the intersection.
I turned and found a woman face down on the sidewalk.
Her arms were tucked neatly at her sides as if she been placed
there, not struck down by a milk crate blown
from the roof of a bagel shop. Everything
about her was crisp and symmetrical. Her green coat
luminous against the red brick sidewalk. I put my hands
on my thighs. I hesitated. Another man knelt
down and took ownership of the situation.
A siren became my permission to leave.
I gave myself permission. I went back to my apartment
above the pharmacy and looked down
on the movie theater. I looked down
at the teenagers on the stone steps surrounding the pillars
with pigeons on them. I considered the old, empty billboard
across the traffic circle. I thought about objects
a coward might paint on it.

I'm a Huge Fan of Anyone Named Ernest Hello

After Ernest Hello

Oh Mt. Haystack, anchor me to the muck
I might be grounded in, the leafy glue
that shall steady me amid arthritis and late June.
    Haystack, palm of lichen and fallen ash limb,
    tether me by my sore knees to the dirt
    I might be balanced semi-ecstatically above.

        May too many of my choices be directed
        by the simplicity of your frailest shadows.
        May my cowardice be apprehended by

your wayward, loosest fog. May I, in whatever
my awe is of your working-class, happy-go-lucky
rockiness, be anything except asinine.
        May my inabilities turn disciplines.
        May my shyness prove conversation starter.
        May I climb without preference for
        particular kinds of crevices or the desire
        for a fake fur baseball cap emblazoned
        with ironic pins and badges.

I'm a Huge Fan of My Wife's Approach to Yahtzee

If that were her ahead of me, the empty gray branches
of what I'd guess are dying sycamores
would be themselves
and not reminders of the shins I saw at Methodist
exposed below her clumsy gown.
The blurry ferns and intermittent lichen
couldn't add a jar of air
to any quadrant of my lungs.
I'd know where I was. The trail
would curve between two somber boulders
and then go down to a patch of sun
where the grass would be littered
with the bark of nearby birches.
If she were here, a snake would square itself
around a little purple mushroom.
A fox would leap into the lake and float along
until it saw a board that made a ramp
into the picnic area.
I wouldn't need to stand beside a sparrow.
The picnic tables would be open.
The restrooms, clean and empty.
Any millipede that I might find would signal
the arrival of a hummingbird. And a hummingbird
means: Roll all five dice again.
Anything we chance to say
should have the swagger of a slogan.

I'm a Huge Fan of Spring

Beside a frail tree, the odor of oatmeal
latches itself to some insects. The sun hasn't gone
entirely down into the shoe
of this long black hill. Everywhere
a damp breeze keeps opening
packages of box plant and leaf litter. Airplanes
and mud hens and gunshots
are scarce. The weekend began
with a single grave-sized cloud advancing
from behind the church and
diminishing by the time
it reached the stadium. It will end
with a half dozen deer looking up
from a pile of mushrooms.

Endeavor in the Manner of the Buddha Raising Her Wine Glass

I know the sea ends. Ten feet up the dull horizon,
a sarcastic mist renounces the presence of anything nautical.
The clouds want nothing to do with the moorings.
The empty patches of sky beyond the oyster
boats are a pale matte gray. It's like they're daring me,
disingenuously, to compare them to a series
of galvanized fluke anchors.
Bewilderment, however, is not the reaction I was expecting
from the outgoing tide. I had always wanted to make
        a toast, but only if it happened
        naturally. I wasn't going to ding my fork
    against a winch or holler "ready about."
    But gradually, in that
        increasingly savory, oyster-scented,
        gray, then blue-gray air, I realized
        I was running out of chances
        to praise my life, so I turned back toward those giant swings
        they use to lower boats into the water and I began to count
        the seagulls on rim of the crumpled blue-green dumpster.

Endeavor in the Manner of the Buddha Going About Things All Wrong

Let me tell you where we are
in this game of Scrabble.
It isn't my turn, but I have already played "festoons."
Outside, the mist ends
somewhere between the porch steps
and the broken Adirondack chair.
The last load of laundry
is already in the dryer.
The screen door is new and a little hard
to open. In the gravel beside the bulkhead,
a pair of hedge clippers
has rusted shut. The wooden handles
turn just out into the clover
below the water spout where
the dandelions are sprouting.
Above my left shoulder, a wasp makes a spiral
in the air outside the bathroom window
where my wife is taking a shower.
Each of these hydrangea blossoms is a little bit
like Dustin Hoffman's head and each of these rabbits
is like an alibi, like proof
I am not taking part in some atrocity
or advocating irreverence. Every robin
that my daughter chases with her bright orange
butterfly net is an answer to the security agent
at the airport who once asked me why
I had a skateboard with the Virgin Mary
on the bottom. I was thirty years old, but she asked me sharply
as if I was a child. I had no
real answer. I bought it because I was alone
and sad. I had time on my hands
and no one to travel with. Mary's posture
seemed to advocate patience
and I loved how the artist made her face
and hands a crestfallen blue. I had forgotten

there were things in this world
that people considered sacred.
At the time, I lied
and said the skateboard was a gift. It took years
to acknowledge it was one.

Endeavor in the Manner of the Buddha Checking Her Cellphone for the Latest Atrocity

The risks are those we have lived with always, the risk
of bringing your diary with you to work,
          of drawing a bulldozer on a birthday card.
          In the distance, the bright bay sheds its birds
          and begins to take on the responsibilities
          of a landscape. A knot of filthy grass traps
                    a plastic bucket near the dock where it bangs
                    against a wooden post repeatedly.
               Your gaze grows from ten different glances.

Anxiety as It Relates to Noon

A genuine haze has culminated
in the branches of the tulip poplars.
A luminous, airy fuzz. A gauze
of loose sun, chimney smoke, and mist.
Take your history with foxes,
and a single fox stands out, a cartoon fox
perhaps, with something off
about its abdomen, or an actual fox
traipsing between a far fence
and the sideline of a football field. In any case,
this is a feeling you are welcome to associate
with orange fur. The psychedelic sparrows
twitch like paisley in the branches
of the poplars. The lids of metal trash cans
glisten where a bored girl leaned
them up against a fence.

Hindsight as It Relates to Reason

November had narrowed also. The sky slimmed
down to a Decembery width, put on
a belt of purple clouds, and started surprising
people with its neon mauve, its hyper-lambent
apricot and coral. When it was time
to go to bed, I would take my socks off
and tie them together. I would lay that bow-like bauble
        at the foot of the radiator and I would try
        to remember to plug in my phone.
        In retrospect, my crucial decisions were made
without my continuing input. I would set a thing
in motion tentatively, and then, when it was time
to weigh and measure how things stood, I would
defer to whatever the circumstances seemed to already imply.
        Whatever the final meaning of those reclining
        silhouettes of naked women that help truckers
        choose their mud flaps, I would lie in bed
        and think about the sadness of their origin.
        I would look down confidently on anyone
        who wasn't scared of owning a guitar.
I would think about the song I started writing
seven years ago and what the chorus might reveal
if I allowed its final goofy phrase to be
repeated like an anthem.

Abstraction as It Relates to Concrete Particulars

By giving herself the task of creating a work that corresponds
to every snowman she encounters this winter, the artist arrives
at a droopy blue shape in the upper-right corner of a painting
called Victory. And by throwing a roll of paper towels
into what's left of the fire, she coaxes a small green squiggle
from a red diagonal smudge. Maybe anvil-like purple shapes
            matter because they conjure
            associations with the loose glass of a lamp post
            I grew up removing a bulb from. Even though purple
            isn't what I felt as a kid when the mail truck
            ran over my bike and my mom came out
as far as the lamp post to agree
            with the mail man that I needed to be
            more careful.
Now, if I could, I'd fold the sky twice
the long way and then also east and west so there
were sixteen sections and clouds
in all but five of them. I would stay
home and read in my chair
by the window and think about the creases
in the sky and what they say about the human
heart. Cars could still catch fire in front
of the laundromat, and old men
            could fall on the sidewalk in front
            of the post office, and ambulances might
            likely still roll through intersections slowly
against the light and almost run us over,
      but if I see a woman
crumpled up beside a drain pipe sobbing,
I won't join the sky that's rushing past her,
I'll ask her if she needs our help,
and when she tells us that her son has
just died, I'll crouch there with my nine-year-old
daughter and let
            our chair-shaped shadows cross. I'll let
                        the present moment be as awful
                                    as a human heart can handle.

Target with Wooden Cubbies for Miscellaneous Ceramics and a Pale-Green Molded Pulp Berry Basket

You can't follow rules you don't know, but you can follow
a moth at least part way through the cemetery.
There are dozens of statues of dogs, and you can gather
wet sticks from the road and lay them across the tops
of their long granite paws. You can imagine
the soul of a dog person smiling.
    If you walk by the court-house, you can feel
    how much of the weather seems to be air exhaled
    by those who have just heard the length
    of their prison sentences. You get the sense
    that the judges feel tricked into ever wanting
        their jobs, that lawyers resent having to hold
        out their non-dominant hand, palm up,
and signal with their fingers
for a binder clip. There are so many steps
in this part of the city.
  After lunch, the way the light is,
  with most of it shredded by all the different poles
  and rods and vents on top of buildings, everything
  could be described as ombré.

Target with Herringbone Bullseye and Alternating Rings of Houndstooth and Mini-Glen Plaid

I was about to add sorrow to my list of pet peeves.
A rabbit laid down in some chives. Grasses
fell over like the fingers of empty gloves. Summer began squeezing
an extraordinary number of cones out of the fir trees.
The neighborhood was changing. Telephone poles
disappeared and in a dream I saw
two telephone poles shoot upward out of the ground
like rockets and impale themselves in a green sun
that was setting behind the auto repair shop.
Prayer was dying out. In the center of
the empty lots between houses, foundations
would appear out of nowhere, and we walked among them
sentimentally as though they were ruins.
It became a thing to gather as many stone
chickens as you could and line them up
beside a garage and make all kinds of plans for them.
It felt less and less good to be alive.
All of the objects (the fuzzy dice, the ceramic fish,
the beach chairs, etc.) seemed to be part of a maze
that was leading to something
more serious, but our thoughts
remained infantile. After dinner we decided
if there were to be any kind of afterlife, you should
get to see where your skull ends up.
If it ends up in a photograph, on a beach
with a crab crawling out of it, we decided
you get dibs on human sorrow.

Target with Rat Trap, Dead Leaves, and Old Tissue

Winter rose up out of a pot of dead grasses
and rustled there, right beside me,
as though the present moment was a stiff,
blond husk trying to get
my attention. The threat of rain had been replaced
with the prospect of wandering thoughtfully
around an unfamiliar neighborhood.
On the dark canal, I saw a sailboat
with a man on it, but it was unclear
how I might get over to that little dock or walk up
to the man and ask him anything earnestly.

Honest Opinion

Andromeda is a weird name for a dog
but a good name for an organization.
I can picture myself behind a clear plastic podium,
smiling like an idiot, saying, "Andromeda has allowed
me to reach my fullest potential."
Maybe we're in the garden of a private museum.
A college student wheels out a bucket of umbrellas
to protect us from the sun. The clumps
of ornamental grasses look like the heads
of shaggy dogs that have overdone it
in the heat, dogs with irresponsible names
like Christopher and Kilty MacMuff.
"With the tools Andromeda has given us," I might continue,
"We can be much more confident at work and making
decisions in the supermarket."
But it's hard to be accurate about where one is
on the ladder of consciousness,
and Andromeda is a feeling one mostly has on vacation,
a feeling no employer could understand, a hunch
that in spring when the kids throw their paper cups
from the sea wall, the incoming tide will carry them around
the pier to where the sandbags divvy up
but do not organize the foam.

More Honest Opinion
(language, violence, brief nudity, smoking)

In a minute or two, new clouds
will test the horizon. Bizarre odors
will divide the field like a labyrinth
of unidentifiable fume. The forest will buzz
with the asthma of wheezing deer, and a memory,
your grandmother handing out
lozenges, will flash over the cracked dish of your mind
and be replaced with an image

of your grandmother topless
filling ice cube trays with bird blood.
Far away, the city is almost empty.
A man is being interviewed about his paintings
on television. As he continues to answer, he has less
and less teeth. He is missing
the first two knuckles of the index finger
on his right hand. He's smoking.
He's talking about "object matter."
When he raises his hand to gesture
and inhale, his pinkie
has disappeared also. "The problem
with dumb motherfuckers," he says,
"They think just 'cause they notice something
it means that it's new."

Even More Honest Opinion

Andromeda is a middle name my mother
and father might have agreed upon.
    It is also a good name for a bee.
    Whatever is deciduous in my desire
    to play a board game called Andromeda might be misdiagnosed
    as evergreen by those who over-advocate for game night.
        The sea is a brine with too much Andromeda in it and the sky
            is an allusion to Andromeda that you verify
            by cross-referencing haystack and pearl.
Whatever Andromeda was before my mother and father
started renting a storage unit, it has only gotten closer to expressing
what comes out as landscape, but is meant as still life with sequin,
grain of salt, and Band-Aid wrapper.
    Andromeda is a small plant you find in peat bogs,
        but it is also the name of a ship
        and a synonym for whatever phrase
        escapes you. If you lean
        out the window, Andromeda
        is where the breeze that hits your forehead
        came from. Andromeda is the despair
            you feel imagining what your father's diary
            might be like if he kept one.
            It is the fat part of an asymmetrical apple,
                the pointy end of an imaginary gland
                that regulates fur growth
                    between the shoulder blades of werewolves.
In a field of alfalfa, Andromeda is a mail carrier
    listening to an audio book of annotated bible verses.
    In a crisis, Andromeda is permission to leave.

You Would Have Enjoyed the Silos

That shade of white, the smug call temporary.
Deer near the edge of the woods look up
at it and tilt their heads skeptically.
The river breeze isn't enough. You could end
a sentence with "because" and no one
would ask you to continue. Yesterday, dusk
felt short, but today this stillness has been gathering
for hours. It isn't even evening.
The grass the mower missed, the grass
that bunches where these silos meet
the ground is stiff and speckled white and suggests
the absence of a supervisor. The men
who chose this color aren't the kind
of men who make a list or tell their guys
to lay a drop cloth down. They aren't
the kind of men who tilt their heads
while looking up at things.

You Would Have Enjoyed the Sermon

I was jealous of the way
the others followed the story, how the boy
could say "coin" and there was
a coin in the yarn of my brain
as if he had handed me something.
Earlier, I had been handed a can
          of beer, a trowel with a purple handle,
          a little bag of metal stakes
          for the tent. Now
          I was given a dying goat with a green scar
          on its cheek, a pail of ancient hammers,
          a broken television.
          It went on like that. We were
sitting around a fire. There were stars
overhead and fish leaping from the reservoir
that lapped at our shoulders. It went on
and on. The boy described
picking a hammer from the large bronze pail
and hiding in the empty cabinet
of an old wooden television set
                         while the city was attacked by
                         farmers. The password
                         was "coin" and you had to decide
                         if you would take all four pills
          yourself or risk an insane asthma
to save your precious goat.
I was jealous of the way
the others followed the story.

You Would Have Enjoyed the Weather

Days I reach the sea count twice.
Once for what the handles of a dune
remind me of, and then again
for what the dune leaves out, the wooden stairs
a sloppy wind-made mound
can't stand for in my fathoming.
On bad days, any boardwalk
is a threshold. The sound of a seagull stabbing
its beak too far below
the gills of a mackerel is the sound
of a lunatic grandfather sorting
a box of old socket wrenches.
On bad days, the horizon is hard
to explain. I feel my panic
soften in a breeze that stops before it fails
to cool another stone.
People who hate hints, hate life amid witch hazel, hate looking
at holly shrubs, hate documentaries about this or that bridge.
The sea air isn't good for them.
If we lived here, fog horns would activate tides in our bladders.
Wind would swing the boats out in the water
so they face the same direction, east.
Between bouts of unintentional glowering, colonoscopies
in adolescence, requests for the introvert
to join in a song, sunlight washes
three sides of a fog.
More time to read is all anybody wants.
Time for the sky to clear. Time for the mud on the road
to reveal itself as stolen sod.
In the city, trespassing is hard, but in a sea town, you climb
a low rock wall and step off into leaves that applaud you.
You kick a half-empty bottle of windshield washer fluid into the tall
dead grass beside the blackberries.
You sit on a pile of branches.

Pamphlet on the Subject of That Which Cannot Be Known

Already this spring I've been startled twice
by what I thought was a raccoon darting out
in front of my car, and both times
it's turned out to be a strong wind helping
a plastic bag free itself from
underneath a dumpster. The landscape
of water wheel and post office
depends for its livelihood on
the way light changes. There are parts
of this town that no one ever sets foot in, cloisters
of gnarled grass that never thrive or die or appear
in any photographs.
There are parts of this town that stand
right next to each other and never touch.
I am thinking of the car wash
and the beer garden, the gargoyle
and the bell tower, the sign
for the bank and the picnic table
chained to the boat.
Yesterday I asked my students what
they were excited about and not one
of them mentioned the landscape. All I could do
was stand there beside a little metal cart
and a pile of miscellaneous power strips
and extension cords. Out the window, a cold helicopter
glistened in an otherwise moth pink sky.
I tried to put my finger on what separated
the wads of green light brushing the side of a dented moving van
from the undulations they landed in and the siren
that leapt from the earth. My students
were excited about getting on with their lives. They were
excited about jumping down steps and shouting
non sequiturs. They were part of the way
light changes and if their leaping
had anything to do with the landscape, it had
to do with what I thought was a screech owl

        on the handlebar of a bicycle
        outside the supermarket. It had to do with
        what might have been a tornado
        between the storage building and my neighbor's balcony,
what might have been a sword in the recycling bin
outside the court house.

Pamphlet on the Subject of Whether or Not You Need a Teacher

It isn't just you who sees
the light outside the deli as a test,
I measure myself against that glittering also.
Sewer caps remind me of eye sockets.
Moonlight flecks the asphalt where it's wet
with beer an old man spilled while waiting
for his bus.
If I find a knife wedged between two bricks
in the side of an apartment building, or what looks like a cap gun
stuck between an electrical box and a lamp post, the strings
of my abdomen tighten around the feathers of what feels
like an impossibly delicate arrow.
I'm baffled by my desire for new kitchen utensils
and bored with my pornographic memory of
women with biblical names. I still imagine myself
inexplicably triumphant and famous for jokes
that every single person thinks of. I forget my friends
have lost sisters and fathers, husbands
and children, and that death is
always recent, incandescent, and awful.
I don't know if you are born yet, or if
your hairstyle matches your mood,
or if you are suffering from something heartbreakingly
specific, but I know you are suffering
in general. I know you are grieving or
in the interval separating two bouts of grief. I know
you are tiptoeing between two
unforeseeable phone calls. I too have held
a cold domino and made plans to put
socks on. I too have sipped expired cider
and been unsure, then sure that it was rancid.
I know you need a teacher.
I know the sky can be freakishly green and that whoever
might offer instruction will fail you. I know
the final lesson is the same for everybody. There is always
one inelegant and shiny detail that disqualifies
your savior as a model.

Pamphlet on the Subject of Light at the End of the Tunnel

It's a lot to lose everything,
but you hear about it often enough.
With so little moonlight left, the fraying
wicker seatback of the rocking chair
barely stands out against the pile of pizza boxes
behind it. You forget how lucky
fortune tellers are, how they can
surprise you just by dressing casually
and not weighing in on things
that can be verified by opening cabinets.
Browsing the landscape for objects that allow them
to say things, fortune tellers are like poets,
they are like people who went to college
to study advertising and discovered ceramics
and now work at an insurance company
editing quarterly reports.
Before I was a landscape poet, I was
a fortune teller and I wore
what you might or might not expect me to wear
if I was seated at a table behind a crystal ball
in a single-panel comic. I thought
I had lost everything, but I had only lost
a number of people who were
dear to me. At dusk, I used to pause
and look up at the women on treadmills
in the gym above the movie theater,
and when I joined the gym above the hardware store
I used to look down at the Christmas trees
discarded between the parked cars
and the frame shop. It didn't occur to me
that I would make eye contact with
a squirrel that a hawk had scooped up
and taken to die on a lamp post. It never occurred to me
that things would get better, then worse,

and then good again, and that I would sit
in that goodness, trying
to apply it to the final bad thing that was headed my way,
trying to ready my eyes for whatever gaze they might meet
looking out from the gym above the temple.

NOTES

The epigraph "the divine wife, the sweet, eternal, perfect comrade" is from "A Song of Joys" by Walt Whitman.

MUSEUM OF HAM

In the fourth section of Seamus Heaney's poem "Singing School," he writes, "I retreated to the cool of the Prado. / Goya's 'Shootings of the Third of May' / Covered a wall – the thrown-up arms / And spasm of the rebel, the helmeted / And knapsacked military, the efficient / Rake of the fusillade." This poem is not an imitation of Heaney's poem, but my retreat to the Prado may have been.

BEWARE OF IDEAS

Writing about *Paradise Lost*, Samuel Johnson said, "The short digressions at the beginning of the third, seventh, and ninth books might doubtless be spared, but superfluities so beautiful who would take away? Or who does not wish that the author of the Iliad had gratified succeeding ages with a little knowledge of himself? Perhaps no passages are more frequently or more attentively read than those extrinsic paragraphs; and, since the end of poetry is pleasure, that cannot be unpoetical with which all are pleased."

ZEN APOLOGY, BEGINNER'S APOLOGY

This poem refers to an article, "'Who am I?' The man who started out as 'Billy Sunshine' may never know," by Eric Russell published on March 31, 2019 in the *Portland Press Herald.*

I'M A HUGE FAN OF ANYONE NAMED ERNEST HELLO

This poem is an imitation of "Prayer to St. Raphael," which is attributed to Ernest Hello by Flannery O'Connor in a letter dated July 14, 1964 in *The Habit of Being*, edited by Sally Fitzgerald.

ACKNOWLEDGMENTS

I am grateful to the editors of the following journals where these poems, sometimes in slightly different versions, were first published:

The Antioch Review: "Flexicore vs. Durastone"

Boog City: "Exile"

The Gettysburg Review: "Man Hitting Golf Balls into a Cemetery," "Youth and Buddhist Activism"

Gulf Coast: "Hospice, North Dakota"

New Letters: "Pamphlet on the Subject of Light at the End of the Tunnel," "Pamphlet on the Subject of Whether or Not You Need a Teacher"

Paterson Literary Review: "Pamphlet on the Subject of That Which Cannot Be Known"

Seneca Review: "Half Day," "Etiquette"

The Southern Review: "Target with Wooden Cubbies for Miscellaneous Ceramics and a Pale-Green Molded Pulp Berry Basket"

Spillway: "Tips to Help You Do Your Best"

Wilderness House Literary Review: "Zen Mound, Beginner's Mound," "Zen Apology, Beginner's Apology," "Zen Wind, Beginner's Wind"

Thank you Cassandra Cleghorn, Kristina Marie Darling, and Jeffrey Levine for choosing to publish this manuscript. Thank you to everyone at Tupelo Press for your support for this book and your enthusiasm for poets and poetry in general.

Thank you Jan Heller Levi, Donna Masini, and Tom Sleigh. Thank you to all of the poets I met at Hunter College who helped me expand and refine my thinking about poetry. Thank you Raf Allison for your comradery and encouragement.

Thank you Matt L. Roar for your general all-around stoke and for assembling Chris, Evan, and Jared who gave me valuable feedback on an early version of this manuscript.

Thank you to everyone who would include themselves in the as-yet-unpublished *Anthology of Early 21st Century Bar Sepia Poets*, especially Aimée DuPont, Suzanne Highland, and Matt Petronzio, my dear friends and essential first readers.

Thank you P.S. 107 Community. Thank you to all of the students over the years who helped me try to answer the question, "What is a poem?"

My deepest gratitude to Steve Tomsik for accepting a cassette tape of me playing guitar and singing into an alarm clock radio twenty-two years ago when we didn't know each other, for doing so without ridicule or visible panic, for agreeing to start a band, for helping me get me the job I've had for the last two decades, for introducing me to May, for officiating our wedding, and for getting us to the hospital six minutes before our daughter was born.

Thank you to my family.

MIKE CARLSON is the author of *Cement Guitar*, which was awarded the Juniper Prize. His poems have appeared in *Antioch Review*, *Gulf Coast*, *New Letters*, *Seneca Review*, *The Southern Review*, and others. He is a teacher at P.S.107 in Brooklyn.